DRABBLE

DRABBLATIONS

By
KEVIN FAGAN

NANTIER · BEALL · MINOUSTCHINE
Publishing inc.
new york

Also Available:
Drabble: Son of Drabble, $9.95
Drabble: Mall Cops, Ducks and Fenderheads, $9.95
One Big Happy: "Should I Spit On Him?", $9.95
One Big Happy: "None Of This Fun Is My Fault!", $9.95
Beetle Bailey: Still Lazy After All These Years, $9.95
(plus $3 P&H 1st item, $1 each addt'l)

NBM has over 150 graphic novels available
Please write for a free color catalog to:
NBM -Dept. S
185 Madison Ave. Ste. 1504
New York, N.Y. 10016

ISBN 1-56163-238-4
©1999 United Feature Syndicate, Inc.
Printed in Canada

5   4   3   2   1

7

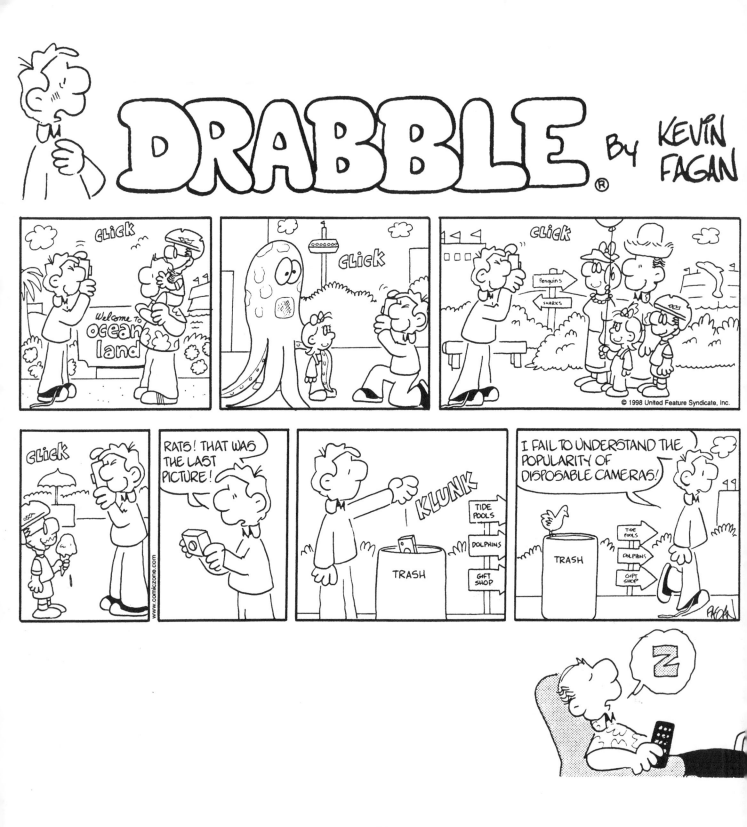

14

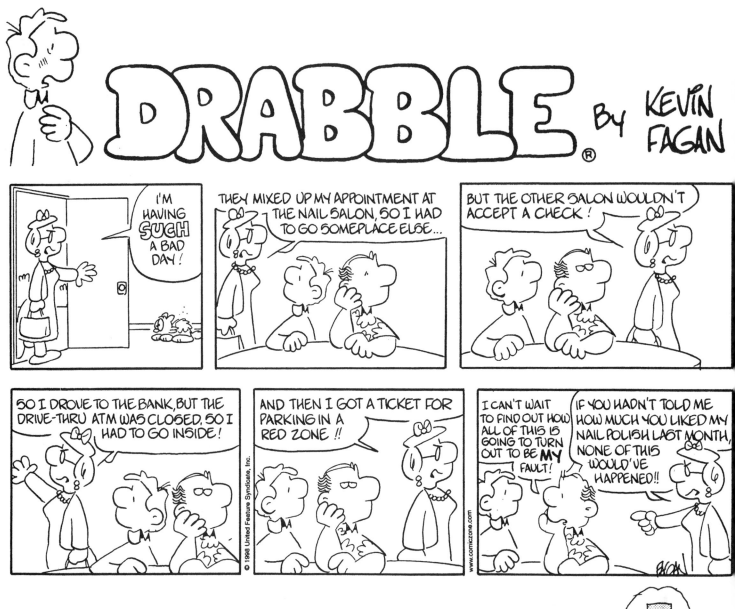

21

23

35

37

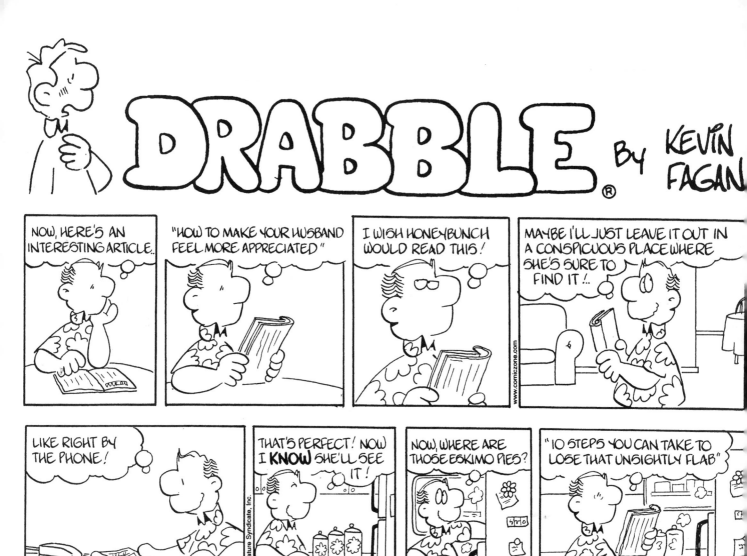

44

45

46

DRABBLE. BY KEVIN FAGAN

DRABBLE by KEVIN FAGAN

LEFTOVER TURKEY!

STUFFING AND CRANBERRY SAUCE!

CHIPS AND DIP!

FIRST DOWN AND TEN!

www.comiczone.com

PUMPKIN PIE AND ICE CREAM!

WHOA... I NEED TO LIE DOWN!

© 1998 United Feature Syndicate, Inc.

THE HOLIDAYS TAKE A LOT OUT OF ME!

THEY ALSO PUT A LOT INTO YOU!

Z

61

DRABBLE by KEVIN FAGAN

90

DRABBLE. BY KEVIN FAGAN

KNOW, NORM, A TRIP TO THE SUPERMARKET OT LIKE THE JOURNEY THROUGH LIFE...

YOU BEGIN WITH AN EMPTY CART, AND YOU CAN FILL IT UP WITH GOOD THINGS OR BAD THINGS.

ALONG THE WAY THERE'S SOME JOY AND SOME ADVERSITY. SOME LAUGHTER, SOME SORROW.

THERE ARE DECISIONS TO BE MADE: PAPER OR PLASTIC? BRAND NAME OR GENERIC?

, WHEN YOUR CART HOLD NO MORE, END UP WITH RYONE ELSE...

© 1992 United Feature Syndicate, Inc.

WAITING IN LINE UNTIL IT'S YOUR TURN TO CHECK OUT!

YOU'RE NEXT, SIR!

TAKE HIM FIRST! I'M TOO YOUNG TO CHECK OUT!!

GROCERY SHOPPING WILL NEVER BE THE SAME AGAIN!

94

95

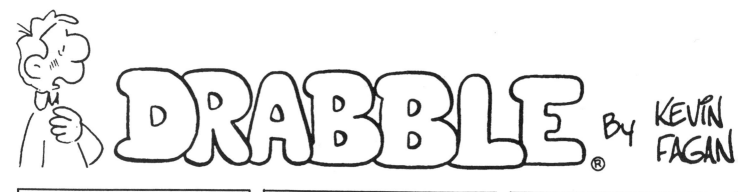

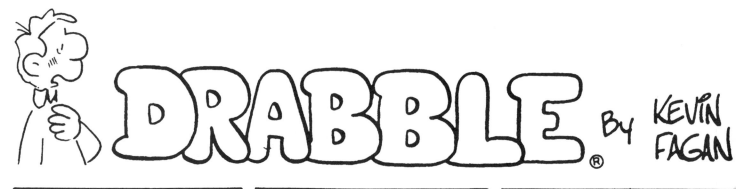

DRABBLE. BY KEVIN FAGAN

HMMM...

YOU KNOW, I'LL BET YOU CAN TELL A LOT ABOUT A FAMILY BY THE COMIC STRIPS THEY HANG ON THEIR REFRIGERATOR.

FOR EXAMPLE...

I JUST NOTICED THAT ALL THE COMIC STRIPS ON OUR REFRIGERATOR SHARE A COMMON THEME...

STUPID HUSBANDS

AND WHAT DOES THAT TELL YOU?

IT TELLS ME WHO HANGS ALL THE COMIC STRIPS ON OUR REFRIGERATOR!

I NEED A MAGNET!

Z

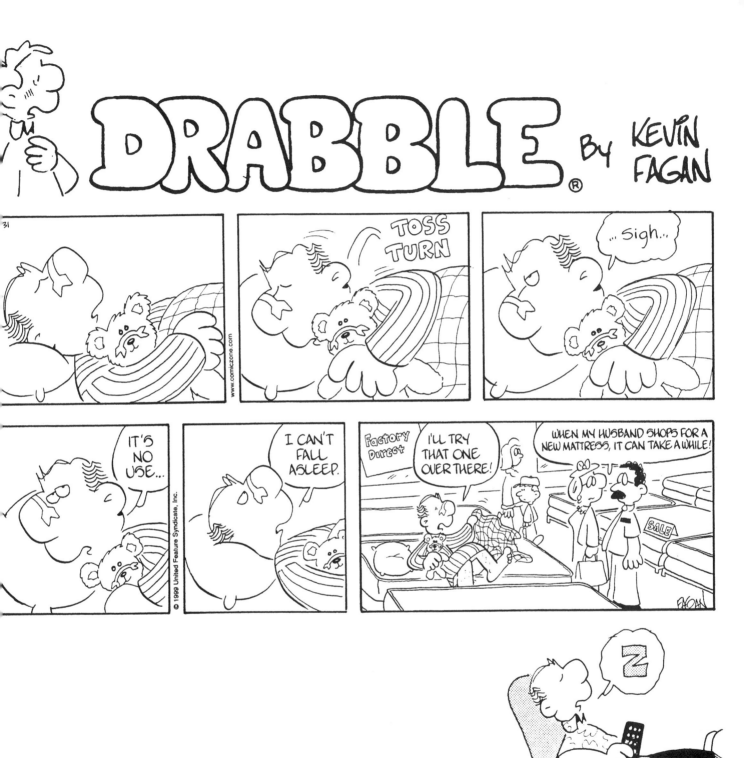

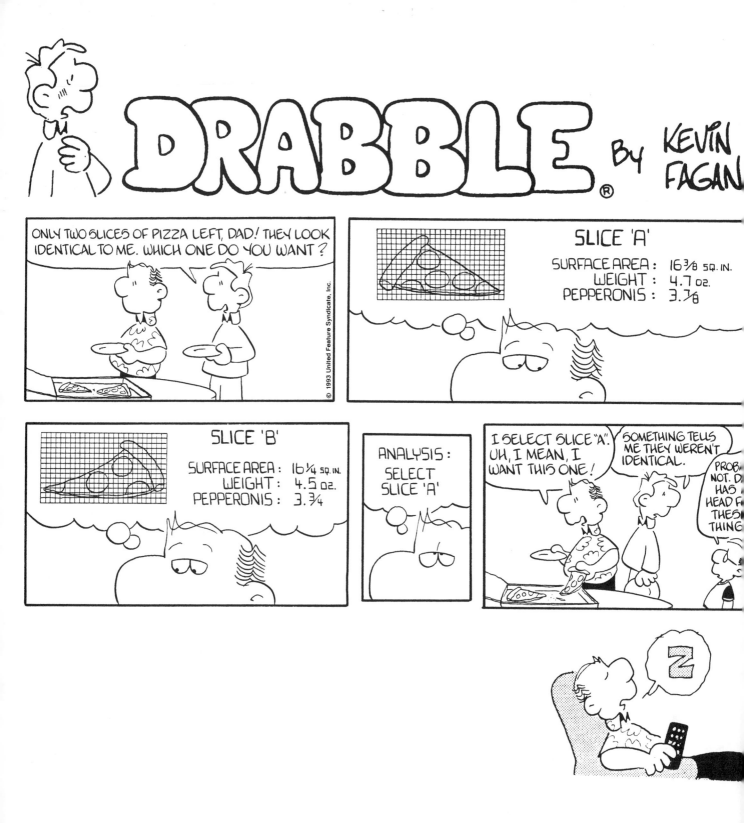